# THE GOWER PENINS

*An illustrated souvenir*

Ymddiriedolaeth
Genedlaethol
National Trust

# Introduction

When approaching Gower from the east, by the M4 or railway, any dismay at the reek of Port Talbot's factories is banished by seeing across Swansea Bay a headland free of industrial clutter. The mud and sand sweeps to Mumbles Head, the Gower Peninsula's southern gate-post. Its counterpart, Loughor, 7 miles north, is also on Swansea's doorstep, but Gower beyond them has escaped development and remains a microcosm of all that is finest in the Welsh landscape. Within its limited compass can be found deep wooded valleys, ancient farmland, lowland heaths and spectacular hills, while its 30-mile coastline enchants with, in turn, salt-marsh, dune-land and golden beaches, rocky headlands guarding secret coves, and marshland backed by tree-clad cliffs.

Gower runs about 14 miles from east to west and is about 7 across. North of Cefn Bryn, its central ridge, a gentle plateau drops to a flat northern shore below cliffs the sea has long deserted. South of the ridge, which is of Old Red Sandstone, the scene is very different. Here limestone cliffs broken with sandy bays face the Atlantic end of the Bristol Channel. The far west is dominated by Rhossili Down, Gower's highest hill, below which Worms Head thrusts another mile out to sea.

Today the Trust holds for permanent preservation more than 10 per cent of Gower, including two-thirds of its coastline. This guide approaches its holdings by tracing a large letter C in an anti-clockwise direction, starting in the peninsula's north-east corner.

Llanrhidian Marsh and Llanrhidian Sands, with Burry Port in the distance on 'mainland' Carmarthenshire

Heathland typical of the Gower interior, with the eastern end of Cefn Bryn beyond

Gower ponies grazing on the north coast marshes

## Gower and the National Trust

The National Trust has had a presence on Gower since 1933, when it was given Thurba Head, south of Rhossili, and by the end of the 1930s had increased that holding to more than 68.8ha (170 acres). In 1954 Bishopston Valley and much of Pennard Cliffs were given, and the next year Notthill, inland from the coast, was given by an elderly lady who had gradually bought it to save it from being built on.

In 1956 the National Parks Commission designated Gower Britain's first Area of Outstanding Natural Beauty. This has held development at bay for over forty years, while the Gower Society has been a tireless champion. Meanwhile the National Trust's interest was fired, and a generous bequest in 1964 enabled it to buy Port Eynon Point, most dramatic of the limestone headlands. When the following year the Trust launched Enterprise Neptune, its campaign to save the coast, the very first purchase was Whiteford Burrows, Gower's northernmost point, a wild region of salt-marsh and whistling dunes of supreme natural history importance. Two years later, Neptune pulled off its master coup by acquiring from the Penrice Estate no less than 17 miles of the Gower coast as well as a number of crucial inland sites.

Corrugated limestone exposed by the waves below Port Eynon Point

(*Right*) A streamside meadow in Bishopston Valley – the idyllic wooded valley which was given in 1954

(*Far right*) Tears Point

Thurba Head, a gift to the National Trust in 1933, was the first property that it owned on Gower

# North Coast

## Llanrhidian Marsh and Welsh Moor

*Cockle Woman*, by Evan Walters, c.1935
(Glynn Vivian Art Gallery
and Museum, Swansea)

Much of the north coast of Gower west of the village of Crofty is owned by the National Trust. The village looks down over Llanrhidian Marsh, a vast area of bird-haunted salt-marsh 6 miles long by up to a mile across, nearly 526ha (1,300 acres) of which belong to the Trust. Beyond, at low tide, the sky is filled with reflected light from a further 4 miles of mud and sand where the estuary of the River Loughor divides Gower from the 'mainland' and the county of Carmarthenshire to the north.

There is a plaintive beauty in the tussocky flats of Llanrhidian Marsh, etched by sinuous muddy creeks (called 'pill' in these parts) and grazed by sheep and shaggy ponies. Llanrhidian's wildlife is strikingly profuse: for this reason the Countryside Council for Wales leases the marshland west of Great Pill and the estuary has been designated a wetland area of international importance.

Besides the wildfowl and shellduck attracted to the grazing, the extensive intertidal mudflats support huge winter roosts of wading birds – oystercatcher, redshank, turnstone and plovers – drawn by the abundance of molluscs, crabs and worms. Boasting some of the biggest cockle beds in the country, this part of Gower has provided a livelihood for generations of human as well as avian cockle fishers. Traditionally, the work of the cockle gatherers was hard, for they followed closely on the ebbing tide to load their flat little pony- or donkey-carts, and many tales are told of pickers and their beasts being overtaken by the rapidly returning tide. Traditionally, too, Crofty was the centre of the industry.

Between Llanrhidian and Crofty, a mile south of the coast road, is Welsh Moor, a wild and beautiful tract of heathland. Unfenced because it is ancient commonland, the Trust's gently undulating property of 59ha (146 acres) runs for about a mile east–west on either side of the road and ½ mile south to coniferous plantations.

Welsh Moor is 1 mile inland from
Llanrhidian Marsh, unfenced until
meeting coniferous plantations

Ponies out to graze
on Llanrhidian Marsh,
etched at low tide
by sinuous muddy creeks

## Whiteford Burrows

To the west of Llanrhidian Marsh an arm of land flings northward towards Burry Port at the end of the mudflats and marshes. This is Whiteford Burrows, a sand promontory more than 3 miles in length, permeated with the scent of sea grasses. Even from a distance the nature of the Burrows is clear, backed by four or five dark patches of coniferous trees. Before it on the nearer east side extend salt-marshes, blending with those of Landimore Marsh, which is in turn an extension of Llanrhidian Marsh; and beyond it lie the tidal flats of Whiteford Sands. To the north, just off Whiteford Point, is a cast-iron lighthouse with elegant iron balconies erected in 1865 (not NT). Standing at high tide in 20 feet (6m) of water, this was decommissioned before 1933. Its replacement was at one time an automatic light on Burry Holms, the island 4 miles south-west.

That the salt-marshes are on land that was once under the sea is evident from the raised cliffs along this coast. The silting process has continued relentlessly within living memory, and it is likely that Weobley Castle (not NT), which commands a cliff-top midway between Llanrhidian and Whiteford Burrows, was in the thirteenth century directly above the sea.

If approaching Whiteford Burrows by bicycle or car, it is best to make for Cwm Ivy, from where there is a footpath up the eastern side, between the salt-marsh and the dunes, and another which crosses the neck of the Burrows parallel to an extension of the landlocked limestone cliff. After threading through a pine plantation, this path reaches the southern end of Whiteford Sands, which continue north for 2 miles to Whiteford Point. Whiteford Burrows is a National Nature Reserve leased to the Countryside Council for Wales.

A particularly splendid view over the salt-marsh and Whiteford Burrows awaits visitors making the ascent of the Bulwark, part of the nearest prominent inland hill. Opposite a thin scattering of houses on the highest point on the road south from Llanmadoc, a track climbs steeply to the west. Following this for 300 yards, we see ahead the ramparts of an Iron Age hill-fort. Part of this fort is owned by the Trust whose land extends also over the common land running north-east. Together with Ryer's Down, the isolated hill a mile south-east, the Bulwark and Llanrhidian Marshes came to the Trust in Neptune's Penrice Estate purchase.

The breathtaking expanse of salt-marsh and dune-land awaiting visitors who make the ascent of the Bulwark

The scent of sea grasses pervades the dune slacks of Whiteford Sands

Looking south over Whiteford Sands, Whiteford Burrows to the left and Cwm Ivy Tor in the middle distance

# West Coast

## Rhossili Down

Dominating the western end of Gower, Rhossili Down at 634 feet (193m) is the highest hill on the peninsula. It is also one of its few features to run north–south rather than east–west. A massive lump of Old Red Sandstone, it appears from below to have been rubbed smooth by millennia of weathering before pulling on its coat of bracken and heather. Beneath this covering lies evidence of a more ancient Gower, for at least seventeen Bronze Age ritual and burial sites have been discovered around the top of Rhossili Down. Many are now reduced to stoney patches beneath the heather, but originally earthen barrows or stone cairns would have covered complex stone structures. Some may have once contained grave goods such as pottery urns, but robbing has long removed all evidence of the people who erected these cairns.

Just below the crest, a little north of the centre, are the remains of two chambers made of substantial stone slabs, called Sweyne's Howes. These are Neolithic burial chambers built by the earliest farmers in Gower between 4,000 and 5,500 years ago. The remains of greatly disturbed stone cairns can be seen around each grave. In later years the area acquired the name of a supposed Viking warlord, Sweyne (Howes being an Old English word for mound). Although it is possible that Sweyne was buried in the area or even within one of the tombs, there can be little doubt that these chambers predate Viking activity in the area by at least 3,000 years.

(*Left*) With its feet in the tide of Rhossili Bay, Rhossili Down rises first to the raised terrace – a narrow coastal plateau above the beach – before sweeping to a height of more than 600 feet (183m). Near the centre of the terrace can be seen the house of the former rectors of Rhossili and Llangennith, whose church has recently been found again beneath the sands of the Warren at the near end of the terrace. The house is now owned by the National Trust and let for holidays.

Rhossili Bay has long been an attraction for surfers, while the Down has now been discovered by enthusiasts for hang-gliding

(*Right*) Just east of the crest of Rhossili Down are the remains of the two burial chambers known as Sweyne's Howes. Although traditionally thought to be the graves of the Viking warlord Sweyne, they in fact date from the Neolithic period more than 4,000 years ago. Pictured here is the best-preserved of the two, which stands to the north

## Rhossili Beach and Raised Terrace

Rhossili Beach

On a good day, Rhossili Down provides spectacular views back over Gower, across to south Pembrokeshire, and over Lundy in the Bristol Channel into Somerset and Devon. Since early historical times there have been strong links across that Channel. Gower was subdued by the Normans in about 1100 and their system of land tenure made Gower a little England, like south Pembrokeshire. Perhaps significantly, thirteenth-century Weobley Castle took a battering in 1406, when 'English' Gower was ravaged by the Welsh patriot Owain Glyndŵr. Although Welsh names account for one in three in Rhossili's earliest parish records, the Welsh language was not spoken in this remote corner at that time. In the late eighteenth and early nineteenth centuries limestone was exported from Gower across the water to improve the acid soils of Exmoor that one can see in fine weather.

Below and west of Rhossili Down sweeps one of the finest bays in Wales – a favourite for surfers and for hang-gliders who launch themselves from the Down. Its 3 miles of golden sands are broken only towards the southern end, by the stark oaken ribs of the barque *Helvetia*, where she was blown ashore on a November night in 1887.

The raised terrace alongside the southern end of the beach, in an area of sand dunes known as the Warren, also covers some interesting features. Although it has always been known that there was once a church on this spot, its graveyard was only finally pinned down at the end of 1979. Parts of the old church were then uncovered by archaeologists, plus the complete outline of a small house and a section of wall, possibly from another house, all totally engulfed in sand. The lost village, believed to date back to pre-Norman times, was abandoned in the early fourteenth century, probably because of a combination of economic decline and gradual encroachment by sand.

The house near the centre of this raised terrace was an old parsonage – Rhossili Rectory (now owned by the National Trust and let for holidays) – and its strip of fields was also church property. The Rector, who was also vicar of Llangennith, either farmed them himself or leased them to a tenant. The present house, rebuilt in the 1850s, stands on a very much earlier site, which it is thought may even have had medieval associations with the Knights of St John.

The wreck of the barque *Helvetia*, driven ashore in November 1887. Rising starkly from the sands of Rhossili Beach, her ribs mock the profile of Worms Head across the bay. The wreck lies close below the Warren, with its buried church, where from time to time the tide, cutting at the churchyard, reveals the bones of long-dead parishioners

## Worms Head

Until the coming of the motor car, the community at this western end of Gower was always isolated. The road from Swansea came to an end at Pitton Cross, so travellers going on to Pitton, Middleton or Rhossili braved a narrow lane, high-banked and muddy and just wide enough for a horse and cart. Thus most inhabitants of these tiny thatched hamlets, or the isolated farmsteads dotted about, were well used to walking long distances to work. Until the 1880s, when a horse omnibus was organised as far as Pitton Cross, people tramped the 18 miles to Swansea. By the 1890s a small school had been established, which served the community until 1969. There was a motor bus running in the early 1920s, and a tractor at work in the fields by 1934.

Worms Head, the mile-long finger probing west from Rhossili, recalls the origins of its name most dramatically at high water. In the $2\frac{1}{2}$ hours either side of low tide one can walk dryshod over the rocks to the grassy eminence of Inner Head, thence across some awkward rocks before the Devil's Bridge – a natural limestone arch – to land on the Middle Head. There are some more rocks to cross before one reaches the Outer Head, the Worms Head itself. When the tide is in, however, all that break the surface are the head and humped coils of a 'wurm' (an Old English word meaning 'dragon' or 'serpent'), trailing its length as it breasts the waves.

(*Right*) A hand-coloured aquatint of Worms Head, published in William Daniell's *A voyage round Great Britain* (1814–25)

The area south-west of Rhossili village contains a rare survival of a medieval open-field system. The Vile, a name thought to derive from the Old English word for field, is divided into narrow strip-shaped fields. Most are enclosed by stone walls, high earth banks or wire fences, but some are divided from their neighbours by low, wide, grassy banks known as 'landshares', which originally surrounded all the strips.

In the medieval period individual holdings consisted of several strips which were not held as a block but scattered throughout the open field. After harvest the villagers grazed their stock over the entire area, relying on natural manure for next year's crop. Gradual enclosure of the strips has preserved their distinctive shape, but by this century most farmers had amalgamated their strips. However, some open strips have survived and can be seen quite clearly. The National Trust has purchased land and covenants in the Vile, thereby ensuring that this rare survival, which is unique in Wales, will be preserved.

Just west of the car-park, the Trust owns a run of three former coastguard cottages, which are now used as a shop, Visitor Centre and holiday cottage.

# South Coast

## Tears Point to Paviland Cliff

Thurba Head,
rising south of Mewslade Bay

(*Below*) East from Thurba Head,
after Mewslade Bay,
fingers of limestone
probe the sea

While many footpaths now drop to the coast, a cliff-top path can take us to Oxwich Bay. Because limestone dissolves under the persuasion of water, the coastline is dotted with caves, and some have revealed to archaeologists the men and animals they sheltered.

Tears Point, an easy walk from Rhossili, marks the western end of Fall and Mewslade bays. This is sandy at low tide below its apron of rocks, and is closed by Thurba Head, which the Trust was given in 1933. A majestic headland, 200 feet (61m) high, it has an Iron Age fort on its summit. The village of Pitton, ½ mile inland, is the nearest approach by road.

If we take the top path, we come to two more promontory forts. These date from the warlike late Iron Age, shortly before the Romans came to Celtic Britain. From Deborah's Hole, high in the cliffs near the first fort, above the inlet noted for a conical rock called the Knave, bones have been recovered and can be seen in

Swansea Museum. More widely celebrated is Paviland Cave (not NT) ½ mile further east, for this is the site of one of Britain's earliest and most celebrated antiquities – the so-called Red Lady of Paviland.

At Paviland in 1823 William Buckland, Professor of Geology at Oxford, found the remains of a mammoth, many implements and a headless skeleton whose bones had been stained with red ochre. Believing that no human could be dated earlier than the Biblical Flood, Buckland – a clergyman – pronounced the skeleton to be that of a woman of the Roman period. He was wrong on both counts. Deposited in the Geology Collection of the Ashmolean Museum, Oxford, his 'lady' is a young man shown by carbon dating to have lived about 24,000 years ago. Paviland Cave is some 30 feet above the sea and only accessible from above for those with rock-climbing skills. The only safe approach is from below at low spring tide.

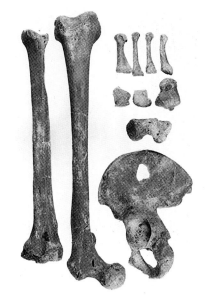

Bones belonging to the 'Red Lady' of Paviland, and (*left*) a 19th-century lithograph from a sketch by Professor William Buckland showing Paviland Cave in cross-section and plan

## Culver Hole and Port Eynon Point

When tundra conditions prevailed in the Palaeolithic Age, and everything to the north was locked under hundreds of feet of ice, the sea level was very much lower than today. Stone Age man, hunting the valley between today's Gower and Somerset, encountered mammoth, cave bear, reindeer and woolly rhinoceros whose remains have all been found in the Gower caves. Warm periods of the later Pleistocene era saw the return of fauna such as hyena, lion and elephant.

Scenically the cliffs between Rhossili and Port Eynon Point are among the finest in Wales, and the cliff-top path shows us their finest aspects. Longhole Cave (not NT), east of Common Cliff, has revealed evidence of Palaeolithic occupation and can be approached by a giddying but exciting footpath. A mile further east is Overton Mere, a pebble beach flanked by Overton Cliff and the bulk of Port Eynon Point. The closest access by road is from the village of Overton, or from Port Eynon itself with its good public parking. The cliff path drops to Culver Hole while continuing over to Port Eynon, though if the tide is out the energetic will want to explore this coast from the rocks below. Either way, Culver Hole is not to be missed. It is the most unusual of all the caves on Gower. A strong masonry wall, pierced with 'windows', rises as if through four or more storeys across a cavern where two rock faces converge. Culver has a legendary notoriety as a castle, pigeon house and smugglers' hide-out, and in some tales as all three together.

(*Above and right*) An exciting – if slightly wobbly – walk over sea-eroded limestone takes us at low tide to below the gully with Culver Hole

(*Left*) Culver Hole, in an angle between rocks on the west side of Port Eynon Point, is a sea cave whose face has been blocked by masonry. This massive wall is pierced with openings, or 'windows', connected on the inside by a flight of stone steps. No doubt associated with the lost castle of Port Eynon, which probably crowned the cliff-top above, the cave has certainly been adapted for keeping pigeons – as is shown by the nesting holes within

## Port Eynon Bay

Of all Gower villages Port Eynon remains most true to the past, with its whitewashed cottages clustered round the church and hugging the lane down to its great sweep of sand. Oyster fishing was a traditional occupation of the community (the wives taking the oars until powerful sailing skiffs were used), together with limestone quarrying, lobstering and crabbing, and smuggling. Indeed, with up to forty skiffs operating, besides local fishing smacks and the limestone boats from Bideford and Barnstaple, the opportunities for smuggling were considered so great that no fewer than eight excise men were stationed in the village.

Beyond the eastern end of Port Eynon Bay, which offers good safe bathing, the Trust's land starts again. Three miles of intertidal rock shelf form a platform below the spectacular limestone cliffs which continue east until round Oxwich Point. The quickest approach by road is to Slade or Oxwich Green from where footpaths lead to the shore, and these also link up with the coastal path which marches over the cliffs to Oxwich. A path from Slade comes in from the north, at the Sands, the only point on this stretch of coast where the rock shelf is relieved by sand. The phenomenon is a circular pool of sand, nearly 300 yards (91.4m) across, cupped on the low-lying rock platform.

Another 2 miles of cliff path take us round Oxwich Point on to cliffs clothed in traditional mixed woods which stretch right down to the village of Oxwich itself.

## Nicholaston Burrows, Great Tor, Penmaen

The Penrice Estate still owns the stretch of Oxwich Bay up to
Nicholaston Pill, the stream which drains the marshes behind the
dunes. Across the pill, all the shoreline round to Three Cliffs Bay,
together with its hinterland, belongs to the Trust. From west to east
this embraces Nicholaston Burrows with their spectacular dunes
beyond Oxwich Bay, the great cliffs behind them peaking to the
headlands called Little Tor and Great Tor, and Three Cliffs Bay
save for a segment beyond Pennard Pill.

Inland from Great Tor are Penmaen Burrows, which drop
eastwards to Three Cliffs Bay. Clockwise, this gentle, sandy plateau
provides the archaeologically minded with a parade of the past: a
medieval ring work once guarded by a tall timber tower; a 'pillow
mound' of the same period where rabbits were bred for their meat
and fur; the remains of a prehistoric burial chamber; and the vestiges
of an early church. But for most of us the main value of the burrows
is the spectacular western flank of Three Cliffs Bay.

## Three Cliffs Bay, Penmaen Common and Notthill

The magic of Three Cliffs Bay enchants all who go there, for it combines the three essential elements of the perfect bay: gleaming sands, majestic rocks and the sea stirring eternally. It derives its name from the row of three tooth-like peaks which stab the air above its eastern cliff.

In its protection of the coastline the Trust has always sought, where possible, to acquire the land behind it as well. For without the hinterland the views from the property are vulnerable. So it was that Enterprise Neptune, when buying Penmaen Burrows on the western approach, also bought Penmaen Common. Although bordering the main A4118 road through Gower, and barely a mile from this heavenly bay, those lofty acres of scrubland at the end of Cefn Bryn can now never be built on. For all time they will survive as the natural backdrop for the views from the coast or cliff land.

Even more remarkable is the story of Notthill – threatened by development, but dramatically saved and presented to the Trust. The 2ha (5 acres) of rocky and bracken-covered hillside at Notthill are in full view of anyone making use of the coastline. Enjoying wide sea views, and even closer to the bay than Penmaen Common, the land had been divided into building lots which were on the market and attracting considerable interest. But in 1955, the year after the Trust gained its first foothold in this part of Gower, the whole of Notthill was presented to it by Miss E. R. Lee, who had doggedly bought it up lot by lot until the entire hillside had been gathered into her generous hands.

(*Right*) Looking east from Great Tor towards Three Cliffs Bay, with Penmaen Burrows in the foreground to the left. Three Cliffs takes its name from the prominent triple-fanged rock on the far side, and the three elements it combines rock mass, water and gleaming sand put it among the most exciting beaches in Wales

## Bacon Hole, Deep Slade and Pwll Du Head

Footpaths again enable keen walkers to cover this stretch on the cliff-tops, while motorists will find paths radiating from the car-park at Southgate, the straggling modern village just above the coast. Fortunately its houses are soon forgotten because these cliffs, which are convex in profile rather than plunging, quickly hide them from sight.

The limestone here is rich in caves, although Fox Hole, the first encountered a few yards from the car-park, does not prepare us for the grandeur to come. Minchin Hole, a short scramble from the car-park, is the largest bone cave on Gower, while the drama of Bacon Hole another $\frac{1}{2}$ mile to the west affects all who are brave enough to descend to its entrance. Minchin Hole, which was first examined in 1850, has been extensively excavated this century. The discovery of three hearths and numerous domestic goods, including cooking pots, bone spoons, combs, bronze brooches and spindle whorls (now lodged in Swansea Museum), suggest occasional occupation during the Iron Age and Roman period. The large number of animal bones at lower levels suggests that animals have also sheltered here over a considerable period. Woolly mammoth and woolly rhinoceros reflect a period when the climate of Britain was much colder. Among other exotic animals indentified are narrow-nosed rhinoceros, elephant, lion and hyena.

Less than a mile west of Pwll Du Head, Bacon Hole takes its name from the red oxide which was thought to make the limestone look like bacon. It has yielded rhinoceros and elephant bones as in Minchin Hole, but also later mammals including the wild ox, or aurochs, and near contemporaries such as the wolf and the modern red deer. East of this cave, below Hunts Farm, the cliffs form a bowl called Deep Slade, while Pwll Du Head, the highest on this coast at 250 feet (76m), is crowned by a cliff-top fort.

The view west
from the limestone cliff land with,
in the distance, Oxwich Point

Towards Pwll Du Head across Hunt's Bay
from the same cliffs above Bacon Hole

## Pwll Du Bay and Bishopston Valley

From the north of Pennard Farm on Pwll Du Head a steep climb descends to a bay of the same name; the 'Black Pool' (which 'Pwll Du' means) is here contained behind a storm beach. Dense scrub on the west side of Pwll Du Bay obscures what was one of the most important quarries on Gower. Quarrying of limestone for use in the building industry or agriculture has been carried out at Pwll Du for many centuries, but the industry reached its peak in the early decades of the nineteenth century. Large stones removed by blasting or chiselling were dragged to the water's edge where they were broken into smaller pieces and piled into heaps on the beach. The present-day storm beach consists largely of these quarried stones.

Most of the limestone was exported to north Devon. At the height of the trade there could be as many as thirty boats in the bay so it is not surprising that there were five inns in the valley. The quarry closed at the turn of the century, but the Beaufort continued as an inn until the 1940s.

From Pwll Du Bay an enchanting 2½-mile walk can be enjoyed up the beautiful Bishopston Valley, which makes a fitting finale to our circuit of Gower. For nowhere else does the peninsula combine such quiet seclusion with its own genuine character.

From the pool to the village of Kittle this narrow valley of cliffs, hanging woods and ever-present water opens a succession of surprises which cannot fail to delight. After experiencing the openness of Gower's salt-marshes and mudflats, its heaths and cliff-tops, the valley might at first appear somewhat tame, like a walk in a park, but it would be wrong to take this valley as a planned landscape. Much of it holds indigenous Gower woodland, with species such as small-leaved lime – rarely found in the wild today – thriving as they did in Wildwood before the Neolithic clearance.

Birds, too, feature strongly here – and with species we might not have encountered until now. Still within sound of the sea we might meet a heron, dippers and a flashing kingfisher, and yellow wagtails flirting along the banks of the Bishopston stream.

Where the cover has suffered from wind-blow, the National Trust replants with native trees. Elsewhere, on the valley floor, scrub vegetation encroaching on the meadow has been cut back to encourage diversity. For the floral richness in this valley combines woodland, pasture and stream-side plants with limestone-loving and maritime species, which typify the diversity of the Gower landscape.

Bishopston Valley,
densely wooded and rich in
limestone-loving plants
and maritime species

Pwll Du Bay,
the Trust's easternmost coastline
in Gower – a view west over the
shingle beach

In contrast to almost everywhere else on Gower, the stream inland from Pwll Du Bay threads a secluded landscape with a gentle character. The Trust's management has included much tree replacement and involves scrub clearance round the meadow edges to encourage the diversification of plant life